IT'S THE AUDITION, STUPID!

IT'S THE AUDITION, STUPID!

The actor's essential guide to surviving the casting and getting the part

Brendan McNamara

It's the audition, stupid!

First published in Great Britain by Pinter & Martin Ltd 2011

Photographs by James McMillan
Design by Klor

ISBN 978-1-905177-28-8

British Library Cataloguing-in-Publication Data
A catalogue record for this book is available from the British Library

Printed in Great Britain by Martins the Printers, Berwick upon Tweed

Pinter & Martin Ltd
6 Effra Parade
London SW2 1PS

www.pinterandmartin.com

To my wife Rachel and my son Toby
& my parents Edward and Mary
Thank you for everything xxx

CONTENTS

FOREWORD

When I held my first casting session I really had no idea what to expect. I quickly realised what a tough job it was to be a casting director and the talent that was needed to be a good one. I only had a few days meeting actor after actor and found it exhausting. You end up repeating yourself, giving the same directions over and over again, trying to keep it fresh for every new actor you meet and for yourself, and it's incredibly hard to do. Yet casting directors do this day in, day out, all week and great casting directors like Brendan McNamara amaze me because they have such incredible stamina and enthusiasm for the job.

Imagine the number of actors a good casting director meets after years and years in the business – actually, you probably don't want to imagine that, it might make you think twice about buying this book! Okay, you're a great actor, or you think you're a great actor, but you're not getting the work you feel you deserve. So what are you doing wrong? What can you do to stand out? As a director I have contact with many actors, some successful, others not so much. But the difference between the great actors that are working and those that are not is negligible. What can separate the successful from the unsuccessful is the quality of the audition, and even great actors, as they know only too well, can still screw it up. The purpose of Brendan's very personal and insightful book is to guide even the most talented of actors over this biggest of hurdles.

Auditions can be very painful, even humiliating experiences for an actor. Brendan successfully navigates you through the minefield of common mistakes that will often cost you the job, simple mistakes that he has witnessed over the years and still continues to see today. I've worked with Brendan McNamara on several projects and believe him to be one of the best and most exciting new casting directors on the UK scene right now. His firsthand knowledge as a jobbing actor, having experienced both success and rejection, gives him a special insight into the audition process.

Brendan genuinely cares about actors. He wants you to do well, not just to serve his own career, but because he finds it frustrating when extremely talented actors aren't getting the work they should be getting simply because they haven't mastered the audition. If you want to be a successful actor, if you really crave that part in a film, play or tv show, then it's imperative that you know your lines but it's equally imperative that you know this book. It's a book full of invaluable and honest advice that could very well make the difference between anonymity and stardom.

Jamie Thraves

WHY I WROTE THIS BOOK

Every day I see the same mistakes in my casting studio. I see very talented actors lose roles, confidence and interest because of misconceptions about what they need to do when they audition. Too many actors share the same misconceptions about acting, the industry and the audition process.

If you're an actor, what you may not realise is that when you do a bad audition, it hurts me too. And when you're kicking yourself afterwards, I'm kicking myself too!

Why? Because when you look bad, I look bad. As a casting director, I want and need you to be brilliant. That's why I wrote this book. I want actors to know that auditioning is all important, and I want you to know how to audition better. I want you to know how to simplify your auditions so that you're not nervous or confused, and I want you to have a deeper understanding of the industry so that you're not handicapped by misinformation.

This book won't give you all the answers because there is no set formula to 100% successful auditioning. What it will do is educate you on the auditioning process, condensing it for you so that you can focus on the important aspects. It will give you insights into what the casting director is looking for and how to give us what we want, and I'll discuss the best ways to prepare. I'll dispell myths about the industry, drama schools and acting and I'll explain why focusing on 'the work' is crucial to your success.

I firmly believe that your audition is the most vital part of what you do as an actor. Good auditioning is what will get you noticed and will get you roles. Hopefully landing those roles will give you fulfilment in your career and life.

MY FIRST AUDITION

I was thirteen years old when Hubbard Casting came to my hometown, Limerick City in Ireland, to cast the Warner Brothers' film *The War of the Buttons*. The producer was David Puttnam and they were holding open auditions.

So I skived off school with my friends and went to the old Theatre Royal where we joined the queue of hundreds and took a number. It was very well organised, with two casting directors doing the auditions in two dressing rooms at the back of the stage while we young hopefuls shuttled from seat to seat in the theatre awaiting our turn. This was long before *X-Factor* or *Britain's Got Talent*, so it was all very new and exciting.

We didn't get any script at this stage. There was just going to be a friendly chat that would be filmed. When I entered the room, I was met by a glamorous redhaired woman named Mary Maguire who seemed very well spoken and very friendly. Before I knew it I was telling her about my family, sports interests and a school play in which I'd had the lead role. I even sang her a few lines from a song in the show.

I remember feeling comfortable just chatting about myself, uninhibited by the camera. Afterwards I was exchanging stories with my friends about what we had been asked to do, and wondering if we would get a 'recall'. A recall! We were already talking like West End professionals.

Looking back now it's funny to think that this, my first ever audition, was probably the best audition I ever did. I was unaffected by ego, pushy parents, drama schools or any false sense of who I was. I didn't want to show the casting director how funny, intelligent or charming I could be. I was simply being me and I was very comfortable being me. I was completely free and ready to be a vessel for whatever the director or casting director wanted.

A few days later I was asked to attend a recall. I remember thinking how convenient this was, as my family were about to head off on holiday and the hotel was on the way. I was met at the hotel by Amy Hubbard who had some scenes for me to look at. This made me nervous as I was not a strong reader and had even attended remedial English classes for a year. But I overcame this with a combination of Amy's helpfulness and lots of practice with the script.

Then I met the Head Casting Director Ros Hubbard. Ros was very nice and chatty at first, just like Mary Maguire, but when we started the scene she became much more stern. I couldn't help but look at the script (even though I thought I'd learned it off by heart) and I felt I was not doing very well because Ros had to correct me and direct me. Suddenly it was like school, and in my imagination Ros had transformed into a strict headmistress and the fun was gone.

I now know what Ros was doing – she was trying to get a good performance, she was trying to get good footage to show her director, she was trying to help me! But it didn't feel like that at the time.

As a novice I didn't understand the process. I felt that because I had been directed so much I was doing a poor audition. When I left I said to my parents "Oh well, that's the end of that then, let's go to Doonbeg". My parents being the great parents they are told me not to worry and to put it down to experience.

Our caravan in Doonbeg was in Tommy Turberty's caravan park. These were the days before mobile phones so when Tommy came down from the pub saying that my sister had called with a message "The fillum people are looking for Brendan!" we all, not surprisingly, got a shock. My mum called Maria and, sure enough, I had to attend another recall in Skibbereen, County Cork. This time it was to audition for the director, John Roberts.

I was a little perplexed about doing another audition. Why did I deserve it when my first recall had gone so badly? We travelled to Skibbereen, getting there early so I could take away the scene and learn it thoroughly. After an hour or so, I went back to the waiting room which was now full of kids.

In my naivety, I thought that they were only casting in Limerick, but in fact they'd been casting in Dublin, Cork, Waterford, Galway, Tralee and London. They had seen thousands of children. Sitting in that waiting room, I suddenly realised the sheer scale of the operation.

Ros came out and worked on the script with me and I learned a lot about acting in those fifteen minutes. She has a fantastic way of getting through to actors, especially child actors. A major part of what a casting director does is putting the actor at ease in order to get the best out of them. I would witness Ros do this again when she was casting *Angela's Ashes*.

I went into a small office room and was introduced to the director, John Roberts. The audition felt fine and I felt confident in what I was doing, which was basically just being myself. When I left and said my goodbyes to the other kids, I wondered if would ever see them again. (I didn't.)

After a week or so, just as I was beginning to forget about the film and focus on a summer of soccer, Ros phoned to say "Have a bag packed – Brendan is very close to being offered a role". This brought great excitement, all that "Ohmygod, Ohmygod!" stuff you see on *X-Factor*. My parents were very excited and I was excited, but more because they were excited.

I now felt under a lot of pressure because I wanted to make my parents proud. Dad noticed I was stressed so he took me for a swim to relax. On the way back, we picked up a film from our local video store. This was where my love of film started, watching movies with Dad. When we got back home Mum and Maria had made a sign in the kitchen saying "Congrats Brendan". I'd got the part! I burst into tears, overcome with excitement, relief and astonishment. This was, after all, a Warner Brothers' film with an Oscar-winning producer. This was my first taste of professional acting, casting and my start in the industry.

PART ONE:

BEFORE THE AUDITION

WHAT YOU'RE LETTING YOURSELF IN FOR

Make no mistake – you have chosen or are about to choose a very tough career. The industry is saturated with actors, there is not enough work for everyone and, to make matters worse, new people join the industry every day.

No other industry has such a poor employment rate: 90 to 95% of actors are unemployed. Of those that do work, 5% make a good living; the other 95% are working other jobs to subsidise their wages. If they just lived on their earnings from acting, they would be below the poverty line.

You are entering a world that can feel like a constant competition that does not end when you get a job. You will feel that you are being constantly judged, that you can't get a break. You may have to do auditions for things you have no interest in just to pay the bills.

You may also be one of those unfortunate people who believes they are talented, interesting, watchable and capable of heartbreaking, heartstopping and heartjumping performances. Maybe your family sees you as a star, or wants you to be a star so they can live the dream vicariously through you, and they've encouraged you and built you up. Maybe you just have bulletproof delusional self-confidence like so many you see on television talent shows. I have seen people like that too who believe that what they are doing is acting, when really . . . really, it's not.

Think long and hard about the life you are choosing. Try and speak to actors who have been there. Don't shut your ears to the horror stories because you need to know them. And you need to know that only a very tiny percentage of the industry makes it to the Hollywood A-list.

This industry is not for everyone. But for all the horror, the heartache and the disappointment, there is hope for you.

Why? Because the industry is so overcrowded with people who should never have dreamed of being actors – you may even have studied with people who should never have been studying drama – you can rise to the top. You can get ahead of the time wasters, the deluded, the downright talentless.

How? By doing the best, most well-prepared, focused auditions you can do.

This can also be a fantastically rewarding career choice. You can work with some of the most incredibly talented, funny and generous people. You can push yourself to discover brilliant things about yourself through inventing characters. You can have that feeling of knowing that the audience is hanging on your every word. You can get that undeniable buzz of seeing yourself on the cinema screen. You can lap up that applause. You can have a life where no day is the same and your dreams and aspirations come true.

DRAMA SCHOOLS

The good, the bad and the ugly

Sometimes drama schools in the UK and Ireland make me cross. I studied at the Beckett Centre in Trinity College, Dublin, and, like most drama schools, it had its good and bad elements. But I'm astounded that you can go to drama school to study acting for three years and only do a week or two of camera acting. Then you leave and 75% of your auditions involve a camera. It beggars belief. They spend more time teaching you how to write a letter to a casting director. Let me tell you, I have never cast anyone because they wrote me a well-structured, witty letter.

The number of actors I meet that have left drama school clueless about camera acting is astonishing. They then go into camera auditions and make a total meal of it. This can greatly affect their confidence, and what's more, it can tarnish the way a casting director sees them. Imagine the scenario. You've recently left drama school brimming with confidence. You pick up an audition for a role in a big budget US movie. It's a chance for you to impress a big name director and casting director. But you're let down by your poor camera acting technique. For some people, an important audition like that only happens once. That may have been your best ever opportunity.

And then there's the 'drama school bubble'. Drama school can be very intense: you are constantly in competition for parts, prestige and recognition. You have people telling you how great you are, or in some cases, not so great. You are being taught about the purity of acting, how to be a vessel, how to give yourself solely to the part. You're acting every day, pushing the boundaries of your ability, going through various emotions with like-minded friends, or even foes.

Then you leave. It's a few months until you get your first professional audition. The voice coaches, acting coaches and theatre history lectures are gone. The level of care and attention you experienced for three years is no more. No-one is talking about how good you were in this play or that piece, no-one is saying you could be so much more if you let yourself go, how they know the brilliance is in you. The social scene is different now. Some people are doing well, some not so good. Some have agents, some don't.

Your agent calls. "Would you audition for a dog food commercial? In a dog suit". Your heart sinks. The bubble has burst.

Don't get stuck in the bubble. Prepare yourself for a very hard time and be prepared to leave the safe place. Your classmates are as clueless as you so don't listen to them. Many lecturers in these schools are also very industry-naive. It's always best to focus on the work. If you're not picking up parts and you've not acted in a few weeks, enrol in an improvisation workshop just to keep the juices flowing.

I always notice the same thing when I visit drama schools, speak to actors about their drama training and think about my own experience. It seems that there is always a drama school sage – usually the head of acting – the one all students want to impress, the one they turn to for advice, the one whose word is gospel. Remember – this person does not have all the answers. This person won't have any great influence when you leave drama school and this person's opinion should be one of many you seek and not the only one.

But for all the bad, there can be a great deal of good in a drama school training. Much of it is down to how you apply yourself. Phonetic studies, voice and accent work are very valuable assets in an actor's career. It can be a time to hone your craft and take risks in a safe environment, because it's pointless playing it too safe in college. You should push yourself and make bold character choices, play unflattering roles and take your time with the characters you have chosen. It can also be a time for you to grow intellectually, learn something about the industry you're getting into and have a lot of fun.

To go or not to go?

This is a question only you can answer. Perhaps if you feel you need a few years to refine your craft, gain skills and even more experience, then drama school may be the right thing for you. But don't forget what I said about the 'drama school bubble'. And that regardless of what the school says, keep your ear to the ground and look out for work in the industry.

You could avoid all financial debt by taking evening courses and/or pursue the other option: learn for real. Get work with your local theatre – I've always felt that repertory theatre was a great way to learn your craft. Throw yourself into fringe theatre or start openly pursuing film work, perhaps as an extra or in short films, anything that can get you credits or experience.

I've met actors who auditioned for drama school for three straight years and still not got in. I've then watched them perform pieces for me and felt they did a good job, and with some guidance and direction could do a great job. What I'm telling you is what I told them: don't let the drama school audition be your last. Some people just don't fit into these schools. Maybe your style is more suited to the camera, so go and flush out the work and let it speak for your ability.

I also firmly believe that having 'trained at' a certain school does not have the gravitas it may once have had on a CV. I can't speak for all casting directors, but I've never paid much attention to it.

Whether you go to drama school or not, it will not stop

your career. If you tread either path diligently with eyes open, ready to learn yet keeping a sense of who you are, both can be equally rewarding.

STARTING OUT

So you wake up one morning and decide to throw caution to the winds: you are going to be an actor. Yet you have no acting experience or credits bar a school play or two. You don't know why, but for some reason this is what you feel you want to do. You have always loved movies, the theatre and you are generally overt in your approach to things. This is what you do.

First, get rid of any glamorous notions you have about yourself or the industry, forget bright lights and red carpets for now because you have a lot of work to do.

Find out what theatres, theatre companies or amateur dramatics are in your area. Call them or write to them to see if they ever hold open auditions, run drama clubs or workshops or need volunteers – anything that will gain you experience and contacts. It's a way in, a start. It's better to be doing something, however amateur, than waiting to be 'discovered'. And you never know who's going to be in the audience. I was once at a local repertory theatre show with my mother-in-law. The cast had no idea that a casting director was there, and had I seen someone of promise, I would definitely have made an approach.

Perhaps you are blessed with a university in the area. Find out if there is a drama department, drama society or film studies department. Student film-makers are always crying out for actors. Write to the film department and let them know you're available for auditions, background work or acting roles and ask them to keep your contact details on file. You will need a headshot – probably not a professional one at this stage, but certainly a picture that clearly represents you.

As I recommend to jobbing actors who aren't getting roles or auditions – it's better to be around the industry in some form than pulling pints in a bar.

The internet is a very valuable resource for an actor. You can search for competitions like the 48 hour one [www.48hourfilm.com], short film postings and all sorts of open film, theatre and television auditions. The Old Vic Theatre in London for example has the Old Vic New Voice open day for new talent and young people looking to start a career in the theatre.* These are the kinds of things that are out there for you, but you have to search for them, they won't jump up and bite you on the bum. Bookmark any useful websites and revisit them frequently for updates and new postings.

You should get a book called *Contacts*, which is published by Spotlight. It's the bible for the UK entertainment industry, with thousands of listings and contact details covering all aspects of film, television, stage and radio.

Now let's say you have built up a few amateur drama credits, some small roles in your local theatre and perhaps a short film too. It may be time to start contacting agents or sending your information (picture + CV) to larger theatre companies.

You could look into registering with Spotlight, The Casting Website or Casting Call Pro. If you do, you will gain access through their sites to information about castings and productions. But before you part with your registration fees, I do recommend that you explore the other free or inexpensive options I have suggested so that at least you have a taste of the industry you are committing yourself to.

Now is the time to get professional 10"x 8" headshots. Shop around for a good deal, and ensure that you have digital copies. This will enable you to email your picture and CV to agents, theatres and casting directors – a much cheaper option than sending hard copies. Always try and save yourself money. We look at as many emailed CVs as hard copy versions.

---

* See Part Four: Resources for more information on this and many other organisations and resources.

Check the websites of the people or companies you are emailing as they may have a preferred format for submissions. But don't fret too much if you get it wrong. We don't have a blacklist in our office of actors who have submitted in a different format that we now won't see, ever.

Your CV should be concise and clear, starting with your contact information, followed by your credits and then your skills. Please double, triple and quadruple check that you have listed your phone number and email address correctly. There is nothing worse for me than calling an actor I'm interested in and finding that the number on their CV is wrong. Don't be caught out by carelessness.

When listing credits, you can be vague about the year of the production. Big gaps can arouse suspicion. But do mention the name of the theatre if it's well known, as this adds gravitas and the eye is drawn to it.

Skills are any useful abilities you have such as foreign languages, driving licence, horse riding and sporting skills. It's good for us to know about any specialist skills like skateboarding, trampoline, juggling.

You should also list any comedy work that you've done, such as stand-up or improvisation classes. Listing any comedic-based work can be very advantageous as casting directors, in my experience, might be nervous about bringing you in for a comic role if there's no sign of it on your CV. The worry for us would be that you're a bit serious and comedy might be lost on you. So if you've done it, list it!

Actors ask me how long a CV should be, or possibly they've been told in drama school to keep it to one page. I think it's best to have your standout credits at the front, but again, you're not going to be blacklisted by all casting directors forever if it's more than a page. If a casting director likes you, they'll get you in regardless.

The covering letter on the other hand should be short and

to the point. I don't have time to read long cover letters. All I am really interested in is your picture and your credits. You'll find examples of an ideal CV template and cover letter in Part Four: Resources.

CONTACTING AGENTS

There are two ways to do this. You can contact every agent in London and see if you get any takers. In my opinion, this could get you mixed up with the wrong kind of agent, but it may also get you a good one.

The other way is to do your research and take advice from actors or any casting director you know about who's hot and who's not. Go to agency websites and make a shortlist. Keep an eye on the sites for announcements that they are taking submissions. If they're not posting this information, write to them to find out more.

I believe the best way to approach agents is to let your work speak for itself. So send a showreel if you have one, or links to your work online or invite them to something you are in. Please get them complimentary tickets – it's terrible to be invited to something and have to pay! Remember, you are trying to build a relationship here.

Don't be too disheartened if they don't attend. Understand that they will have a lot of invites to shows as well as looking after their current clients. You're also up against all the drama schools and everyone else who's looking for an agent.

Focus on the work. You never know who else might be in the crowd. But if you've had nice replies to your invites, email updates on your progress and invite them to the next project.

Having an agent is a luxury not a necessity. An agent can only do so much, and YOU are still in charge of your own promotion. Don't stop pushing yourself just because you have an agent, and don't feel you have to commit to the first agent that comes along. Take your time and be sure that you have a good level of communication with your agent before handing them partial control of your career.

CONTACTING CASTING DIRECTORS

Approaching casting directors is similar to approaching agents, and I think it's a better option. You should try and contact every casting director you can. Again, let the work speak for itself by sending showreels or invites to something you're appearing in.

Don't be disheartened if they don't show or don't reply – agents, actors and drama schools are all vying for attention. If you do get a response then build on the relationship. Obviously don't bombard the poor casting director with weekly emails, but drop them a quick line every couple of months if there's something they can see you in. Keep your letters or emails pleasant, short and to the point.

Believe it or not we do watch showreels and review or file the CVs we are sent. I like nothing better than an email with a link to a showreel – YouTube is a godsend for actors. And it's easier than having to store hard copies (but just so as you know, I don't mind getting hard copies).

That's basically it. Forget the glitz and the glamour. Like any business you have to get your name out there and you have to get experience. No one really becomes a star overnight. Check out the backstory and career progression of any actor you can think of and you'll almost certainly discover a long journey to the top. Everyone pays their dues.

KINDS OF AUDITIONS

There are several different kinds of auditions. They may be dictated by the director's style or the project type or the budget. Here are some general guidelines.

Theatre

Theatre auditions usually take place in a theatre space. You might be asked to prepare a section from the script and to bring your own monologue. If you are auditioning in a large theatre space, try to warm up your voice in the waiting area or outside. Your performance will be affected if your voice is cold and can't fill the space. If the director and producer hear that you are straining your voice, they may well wonder if you can stand the pace of a full professional run. So don't just sit in the waiting room getting tired and bored – do a warm-up.

Be sure that you are comfortable with your monologue and change it every now and again to keep it fresh. If you're bored with it, why should we be interested in it? Try and pick a monologue that's in keeping with the piece you're auditioning for. Don't always go for the big emotional tearjerking stuff as you will be one of many who make this choice, and the idea is to stand out. Something a bit more lighthearted and colourful may well give you a better chance.

Don't come with a fully formed idea of the character – let the director guide you into it. They need to know that they can direct you, and while having a few ideas is nice, don't be too fixed or rigid.

If for whatever reason you find that you're having the audition in an office space or small space, adjust your delivery accordingly. You don't want to appear to be overacting. It's a good idea to discuss this with the director – say that you're bringing it down to suit the space. And it's always good to ask a question.

As with all auditions, you should learn the script. You will be working against yourself if you don't. The producer and director will inevitably wonder why you haven't learned it and whether this is going to be a problem throughout rehearsals. So don't put that doubt in their heads, don't make life harder for yourself. The bottom line is prepare and learn . . . learn . . . learn the script.

And again, as with all auditions, do your research. Research the people you are meeting, the play you are reading and the theatre company involved. Like film directors and film production companies, the theatre director and theatre company will have a certain style. Being aware of what that is will help you pitch your audition and may also help choose the material you decide to perform.

Commercial Auditions

Commercial auditions can be fast and very random. You can sometimes leave wondering "What just happened there?" They usually take place in a casting studio and will be recorded on camera so that a shortlist can be sent to the advertising agency who in turn will take it to their client.

You may be asked to do something that is in the script, you may be asked to improvise or you may be asked to do something totally random. Just embrace it and go along with what the director has asked for.

In advertising, product is king and you, I am sorry to say, are merely a catalyst for the company to get their message across. This should inform your audition – it's not that you have to perform as if you're on QVC, but you need to remember that it's all about selling products. The people making the decisions will be looking at how well you fit into the campaign.

If you're asked to read dialogue, stick to the script as closely as possible. In most cases, the scripts will have been approved down to the last comma by the ad agency and the client and what you're reading is what will appear in the finished commercial. If you go off at a tangent to demonstrate your range, we probably won't be able to show that footage to the client, who has paid a great deal of money to see something very specific. This also applies to improvisation – keep it simple and close to the script. Don't be afraid to ask questions if you don't understand something as you can't possibly do it well if you don't know what it is you're supposed to be doing.

TV and Film Auditions

It depends on the budget and role being cast, but these are generally a lot more relaxed than commercial auditions. However, that's no excuse to let your guard down.

You will usually be seated opposite a camera and the director or casting director will probably just chat with you about the project and the character.

This is so that we can focus on you and the dialogue. Recalls or full screentests may be more detailed and involve wardrobe, hair and makeup and other actors. Big budget films may do a full on film set screen test.

Some film directors love to start the casting with an improvisation. Others will also do this, but won't record it, then they'll bring you back and hand you a script. Whatever the variation, you just need to focus on what you're being asked to do, and learn, learn, learn that script!

Open Auditions

Open auditions are often held for feature films where the director is looking for new young talent, raw talent, specific ethnic types or an ultra-natural feel for the project. The auditions are usually open to the general public but can still impose some strict criteria in regard to age, weight and so on.

They can take place in hotels, town halls or concert arenas. You may be asked just to talk about yourself or you could be asked to do a small piece of script. The waiting can be long and tiring, so bring a book and a bottle of water.

Musical Auditions

These can be similar to theatre auditions, but it's likely that you will be asked to prepare a song and be accompanied by a pianist. As always, think about the material you choose to perform. Don't choose anything you are bored to tears with, think about the show you are auditioning for and let it inform your decision.

Musical auditions will often be an all-day affair. You might have a dance workshop in the morning and then be asked to come back in the afternoon to focus on singing or acting, and then you may be asked to return for an evening session. It can be a gruelling process, but being a cast member in a musical can be very tough: eight shows a week singing and dancing can take its toll.

PART TWO:

THE AUDITION

THE CALL

Your agent calls, or if you don't have an agent then the casting director may call you directly. These are the first questions you should ask:

1. Who is the director?
2. Is there a script I can see beforehand?
3. Who is the production company?
4. If it's a commercial, what's the product? If it's a TV audition, what's the programme?
5. Is any particular dress required, eg suit, evening dress, tracksuit?
6. What are the dates of the shoot?

There are many reasons why you should find out who the director is, and you would be surprised at the number of people who don't ask these basic questions, turn up to auditions ill prepared and then wonder why they don't get the gig.

Directors, like musicians or painters, have a style of working. If you do an online search, you should find a showreel or credits that will give you a good indication of how this director works. Whenever I am sent a script, I will google the director, examine the credits, watch clips on the showreel or try and find footage of the film and tv credits.

Once you watch a director's showreel, his or her style can become more apparent and the script can start to make more sense. If you can't find out the name of the director or there is no showreel, then check the production company's website. They may have previous commercials from an ad campaign or clips from a tv programme. This can all help you to prepare for the audition and give clues as to how to approach the script.

As actors you should be watching everything you possibly can, be it movies, theatre, tv or commercials.

Having a good knowledge of the industry can really enhance your ability to do well in auditions. After the success of *The Office*, for example, a lot of directors wanted to shoot their commercials in that same 'real' or 'natural' comic style. I can't begin to tell you how many times I was sent casting briefs that said "must be real and natural comic performances like *The Office*". If you're looking at a director's work and it's all about natural, understated performances, there's a very good chance that this is how you should pitch the audition. If it's all slapstick and heightened performance then take this into consideration, but remember that a heightened performance on camera is very different to one on stage. We'll revisit the dangers of overacting or heightened performance throughout the book.

I may bring in anything from eight to 28 actors for a single role. If you have taken the time to do a little research and think about your performance you are already ahead of the game. That's what it's all about – getting onto a shortlist, getting recalled, pencilled and more importantly, remembered.

I guarantee that at least a third of the other performers auditioning will not have prepared the script properly, won't be dressed appropriately and will not even know who they're meeting. When I looked after reception at Coptic Studios in London, I was shocked by the number of actors who didn't even know the name of the project or product they were auditioning for, let alone the name of the director. You, by being prepared, will have already put yourself into the top part of the pack, and that's without even attending the casting.

The industry is full of weekend warriors who call themselves actors. These are the 'performers' (and I use the word loosely) who turn up to auditions unprepared. Some of these people can fake it and make a career from it, but the majority can't and they end up disillusioned with their agents, their training, the industry and themselves. These are the kind of performers who turn round in a commercial audition and say "God, this script is a bit naff!" while the two creatives who have been working on the 'naff' script for the last six months are sitting there thinking "riiight . . . so we won't be working with you then". It sounds like an apocryphal tale but it actually happens, and there are plenty of similar instances where actors have shot themselves in the foot before uttering a word for the audition.

These are the performers that blame even the hardest working agents for not getting parts or auditions. Not bothering to find out the relevant information about your audition is an easy way to handicap yourself before you've even entered the casting studio. It's up to you to get this information from your agent. If you don't take your audition seriously, why should anyone take you seriously?

Something that's not often realised is that casting directors cast across the board. I could be casting a mundane internet commercial one week, then the following week I'm casting a tv pilot or a feature film. If I've met you and seen a good, well-prepared audition, then I'm happy to see you again because I know I can trust you.

Here's a good example. I was casting an internet campaign for MBNA a few years ago and two girls were pencilled. Both these girls came dressed as requested and had prepared a fantastic comic character based on the brief I sent to their agents. Obviously, one got the role and the other didn't, but when I was casting a pilot for the BBC a couple of months later, they were top of my list to audition. This is the basic principle of this book: good, interesting and well-prepared auditions will progress your career, and by treating all auditions with the same respect, you may find that a little commercial leads to bigger and better projects.

Casting directors remember the good people and we

bring these people in because we know they can be trusted to bring something special to the audition. We take note of the good people who are pencilled and even those who are not. Sometimes I disagree with my client as to what constitutes a good performance, and I'll want to see that actor again because I think they have talent and may be right for another role or project.

As far as I'm concerned, your job is to make me look good. But if you've come to my casting and given a poor audition because you're unprepared or because you can't be bothered or you won't take direction, then I look unprofessional for inviting you in the first place. If you make me look bad in an audition, then I guarantee that you will never darken my door again. I believe this to be the case with most casting directors.

What's more, if I look bad in front of my director and producer, then they may go somewhere else with their next project. I have enough competition out there without having actors throwing a spanner in the works.

Your audition is an advertisement for you and your craft. If you don't take your audition seriously, then it's a poor advertisement for you. Even a 30-second commercial for what you may consider to be the most mundane product with the most boring script could be an opportunity to meet and work with good people. Sir Alan Parker, Ridley Scott and David Fincher all started as commercial directors. David Lynch, Spike Jonze, Wes Anderson and Ang Lee head a long list of movie directors who've shot commercials.

Okay, perhaps a part in a commercial doesn't really satisfy your artistic ambitions but at the very least it may pay the rent. Doing a good audition and getting the part is also a great boost to your confidence. And it's a professional credit on a CV that may be overladen with student and amateur work.

Another recurring actor myth is that casting directors, directors, agents and producers are all in some way stopping you from being your best.

Believe me, everybody in that casting studio wants you to be brilliant. I want everyone who comes to meet me to be so fantastic that my director has a sleepless night deciding who to cast. If a director has a tough choice or a lot of options, then I have done my job and they will use me again. If a director can get a great performance out of you, then the project will be all the better for it and the production company will want to use that director again. And if your performance has enhanced the project, the production company will be employed again by the advertising agency, tv company or studio. This is how it works. As an actor you are a small part of a large machine.

Anthony Hopkins once said "An actor's job is to show up knowing their lines". This may be an oversimplification, but in so many cases, it's very true. If you have prepared for audition well, then we know you can be trusted with the role, whether it's a one-day gig or a six-week shoot. I've held recall sessions for tv series regulars and actors have turned up not knowing their lines. The producers were appalled and I was highly embarrassed. The actors who eventually secured the parts in the series were the actors who had bothered to learn the script. And that's because they could present themselves better on camera and thus gave a better audition.

Think about it. It's a camera audition. We don't want to see the top of your head while you search for the line in the script. We want to see you.

Actors who say "I didn't know we had to learn it" drive me to distraction. Of course you have to learn it! I mean, really, if I want someone just to come and read the script I could ask any person on the street. If you've spent adequate time with the script, you should be off the page, no excuses.

Remember too that we have to show your audition to the film and tv executives, the ad agency people and their client. They need to see the best of you on that tape and, trust me, sight reading is not a good look.

Auditions are nervewracking for actors at the best of times, but if you have learned your lines, then that's one less thing to worry about. When you're off the page and well prepared you can take direction better and your audition will look better when we review the tape. Every director wants you to have learned your lines, even though they're smiling and saying it's okay if you haven't.

As a casting director, I don't make the final decision as to who gets the part. Sometimes the director and producer don't make the final decision. The people who make the final decision are often not even in the room. The people who make those decisions are the studio executives, the tv commissioners or the heads of marketing departments. What happens is that the director or the ad agency will go to these people with a short list and recommendations. They will fight your corner to get you cast, but you have to give them something they want to fight for. So be prepared. Deliver an interesting, well thought out audition which will give them a reason to say "This person is great, I want to cast them."

You may not realise that this industry is deadly serious. Alright, so we don't usually wear suits and there's a lot of joking around but directors and producers are serious people. There's usually a large amount of money involved and strict deadlines to meet. Directors are serious about their showreels and producers have to be concerned about their directors' output.

Now I know that occasionally your poor agent won't have all the relevant information and maybe that's my fault. Sometimes the casting briefs are late, or we're not allowed to email it or the script is being rewritten and will only be available on the day of the audition. There are ways around this if you think ahead, like arriving early to give yourself enough time to look at the script and having a quick word with the receptionist to see if there's any other information you should be aware of.

More often than not, the casting briefs we send to your agent will have all the information you need. I always do my best to include everything that's relevant, and any other casting company I've ever worked for did the same.

RECAP

- be prepared
- ask basic questions about the audition
- research the director's work
- treat all auditions with respect
- learn the script

AUDITION PREP

Preparing a script is not only vital to the success of the audition but is also an advertisement for your craft and professionalism.

Remember that this is all we see! We don't have time to investigate the very depths of your ability, creativity or intellect. We don't have time to imagine what the script would have been like had you prepared it. We need to see that you can do what you're being asked to do, with professionalism and good acting ability.

Some actors in preparing a script fall prey to 'overpreparing' a scene. Don't get me wrong, you can never prepare enough, but this is what can sometimes happen. They get a script and think "This is great, I could do this and that with it." They think about the scene and start learning it, using their ideas to hit the beat they are inventing for themselves, getting the emotion of the scene, really feeling it. It's all very noble and might even work occasionally if the director likes what is being done. But what I see happening a lot is that if actors have learned the script one way, they find it very difficult to change it on the next take. They're locked into it.

I'll prove this to you. Think about your old drama school monologues, dust one of them off and deliver a few lines from it. I'm willing to bet you delivered it in exactly the same way you did at drama school. Now try the same monologue but change the setting to a pub, change the era, pause in different places, add some laughs. Was it difficult to break away from the style in which you'd originally learned it?

Learning a script in just one fashion can be counterproductive and restrictive to an actor when auditioning. If you do one take and then you're asked to do another differently, and you keep hitting the phrases in the same way and can't take the direction given, then the game is up.

When preparing a script or scene, I recommend learning it in as many different ways as you can think of. Try the scene with a funny voice, try it fast and slow, try changing your gender, try anything you like. Learn the script but don't just learn it in one way only because you think it's good or you think that's how it should be. You can never know exactly how a director will want to play a scene, a pause, a phrase. If you learn the script in this fashion by using lots of varied deliveries you will find that you are free and easy with the dialogue. When it comes to the audition you will be better able to take direction, and that's what really matters here. Directors need to know that you can take direction.

And now, what to wear? The eternal question that we ask ourselves throughout our lives. As an actor, you may have to ask this question more than most. Dressing appropriately for the audition is of utmost importance, and probably one of the most common mistakes made by actors.

It's not about 'looking your best'. Here's a good example: the script reads 'Elise is a hardworking nurse coming off a 15-hour shift'. Now why would you dress in your Saturday night finery for this role? Yet this is what I see, female actors who ignore the script and dress like they're going out on a date because they feel it represents them better. It would be much more in keeping with the character of the nurse to wear minimal makeup, tie the hair back and wear something plain and basic.

If you say "I need to feel comfortable if I'm going to do a good audition", I'm going to disagree with you. Acting is not about you being comfortable, it's about the character you're inventing for us.

Men have a similar problem. One man's casual can be another man's smart – and vice versa. Examine the script for clues about style of dress. If the script is vague, google the product or tv show. Chances are there'll be something on the internet to inform you. Carlsberg's "We don't do ________ but if we did, they'd probably be the best ________ in the world" campaign always featured normal lads in shirts, jeans and trainers. If you're auditioning for a similarly blokey lager commercial, it's probably best not to turn up in your favourite skinny jeans, Poste No Point loafers, scarf and new romantic fringe.

I always recommend dressing for the part, but I'm always hearing actors saying that they didn't want to appear 'too keen'. Sorry, but this is drivel and it's lazy. You won't appear too keen, you're going to look like someone who has put some thought into your appearance and not turned up looking out of place.

What about an audition for a period costume piece? There are plenty of subtle things you could do here, with your hairstyle for example, or wearing something vintage, a retro look blouse or top.

If you're auditioning for a waiter, wear black trousers and a white shirt. If the character is a bank manager, wear a suit. Why? Because when our client is looking back at the footage they will instantly see the character, and then you are halfway to being cast. No matter how hard the director and I fight on your behalf, if the client can't see it or doesn't have the time or inclination to visualise you in the part, then chances are you won't get it. Wearing something that hints at the character is very strong and will help those clients with little or no imagination.

So help yourself to help us cast you. Give us that help, that nudge, by dressing in the right manner because you've prepared thoughtfully. Again, you will be ahead of the game and ahead of others who haven't made any such effort. You will get onto that shortlist and you will etch yourself into the brain of the casting director.

An American actress told me this story during one of my lectures. She had auditioned for a nationwide tv ad campaign in the USA for an orange fruit company, and it promised to be very financially rewarding. She and another actress were recalled four times – just the two of them. Each time she wore the same outfit because she thought it was a safe choice. When her agent called to say that they wanted to see her yet again, she rightly asked if there were any new notes – did they want her to do anything different, wear anything different? Her agent said there were no new notes and to wear the same outfit as before for safety, also that this might not be the last recall.

She was keen to land the lucrative role, thought about the audition and talked about it with a friend who suggested she wear an orange dress next time. She resisted at first, but then thought why not give it a go? It may work as a visual aid or something and the situation was probably in the lap of the gods by this point. So she wore a summery orange dress to the next recall, and the actress she was competing with wore the same outfit as before. The orange dress tipped the balance in her favour, and she landed the part.

When I was working on a Jaffa Oranges campaign here in the UK, I met the head of Jaffa, a lovely man who talked about nothing else but oranges. The stream of facts and anecdotes was endless. But that's how it is. Put four actors in a room and they'll talk about the industry. Put four phone executives together and they'll talk about phones. It's what we do, we talk about work. So when you're auditioning for a commercial, remember that the product is king and regardless of how great and funny you are, it's still all about the product.

Good research is invaluable before an audition. As an actor today you are blessed with resources like the internet and google. Good research can really help your confidence, and if you're asked a question or for your opinion, you can show knowledge and the fact that you've taken the time to prepare.

RECAP

- beware of 'overpreparing'
- learn the script, but don't lock yourself into one style of delivery
- directors need to know you can take direction
- dress appropriately for the audition
- do your research

THE WAITING ROOM

This may seem like a non-issue for some of you but the waiting room is an important part of your audition preparation. Many roles are lost in the waiting room before any text is uttered.

The time spent by actors in the waiting room is the most abused and wasted time in the whole process. I can't tell you the number of occasions I've looked out from the studio into the waiting room and seen actors chatting, their poorly prepared scripts lying on the seats beside them,

To make matters worse, the first thing they say when they come into the studio is "I just got the script". Actors sometimes say this even if I've sent the script out days ago – it's like a kneejerk reaction to entering a casting studio. You're apologising for your audition before you've even started and you're telling us that you're not prepared. It's like a photographer saying "I haven't read the instruction manual for this camera, so I'll just take a shot and see how it goes".

You're starting your audition by apologising for your craft, as if you're worried that you're going to be judged on memory rather than your acting ability. If we've delayed you for 45 minutes, then we know you've had 45 minutes to learn it. Starting your audition like this weakens you and makes you seem unprofessional.

If the audition is overrunning, use your time in the waiting room to prepare your script and get yourself focused. If you were at the National Theatre waiting in the wings to go on, you would be preparing yourself, 'being in the moment' and focusing on your entrance. You can 'be in the moment' for a commercial, tv or film audition. Why waste your own time in the waiting room chatting to old drama school mates? They're not going to get you a job and you can catch up later, in your own time. The audition is your place of work.

Let's make it even more practical. Getting around can be expensive. You've paid to travel to your audition and you may even be taking time off from your other job, which is costing you even more money. Don't fritter away your time and money for the sake of a chat in the waiting room. This industry is full of weekend warriors and lazy actors who are not committed to their craft. Do not let your time be wasted by these people.

I'm not asking you to turn into a robot but you really need to be concentrating on the material at hand and not moaning about how slow the industry is at the moment or how reality tv is stealing all your parts. If you start socialising in the waiting room, you will lose focus.

Casting at its most basic is a job interview: you are there to get a job. In any other industry, if you were attending a job interview you would not be sitting in reception nattering or entertaining the other candidates. You would be thinking about good questions to ask, making notes and rehearsing your answers. Treat your audition with the same respect you would give to a job interview in any other industry.

When I was freelancing out of Coptic Studios, John Hubbard brought me in to operate the camera at Ron Howard's casting session for *The Da Vinci Code*. Jared Harris (son of Richard) was auditioning and the first thing that Ron Howard said to him was "Bryce says thanks for the notes". Afterwards I asked Ron what these notes were and he said that when Bryce (Dallas Howard) was starting out in acting, she found the waiting room to be a very nervy, bitchy place. She couldn't focus on the script and she felt she was doing badly in auditions because of this. She spoke to Jared about this and his advice was simple but very effective "Get out of the room . . . get out of the room". Very simple. Very effective.

If you arrive at an audition and someone strikes up a conversation or starts flirting with you, or you think that everyone else looks better, prettier and funnier than you or there's a baby casting going on and babies are crying and kids are running around . . . GET. OUT. OF. THE. ROOM. Just tell the receptionist that you are outside. Don't worry, it's in our interests to come and get you because we're the ones who look bad if you don't turn up. Take control – it's your audition, your career and your craft.

Get out of the room so that you can learn, practise and focus on the script. It will help you to shake off that bad train journey, enable you to put comments from other actors out of your head. Auditions are tough enough without having to deal with unnecessary distractions in the waiting room.

Another thing that can happen is that you start thinking everyone is more attractive than you, or you wonder why everyone else seems to have shorter hair or whatever. You need to ignore everyone and everything and focus on the task ahead of you. You are there for a reason, be it your CV or photograph or the fact that the casting director has seen you in something and likes your work. If you let yourself start worrying about everyone else, you will lose confidence and focus. And unless you are focused on what you are doing you cannot hope to do well.

An actor in one of my workshops told me this story. He was in the waiting room at a commercial audition and noticed that he was the only guy with a shaved head. Everyone else had floppy hair. He thought "God, they've seen an old photo and there's been a mistake – nobody told them my head was shaved". He thought about leaving, then decided to go in to the audition anyway and give it everything he'd got. He got the part because his ability shone through, to the extent that the original casting brief was re-thought. So don't worry about anyone else in the waiting room or what they look like.

When I am preparing a casting, let's say I plan to bring in twelve people. Of these, maybe nine or ten will be right on or close to the brief, but two or three will be 'wild cards'. These are usually actors I have met before, seen in the theatre or on tv, actors who have done good work and auditions. They may be totally off brief, but I include them to get the director thinking. They can be a breath of fresh air after seeing a number of actors with similar features and accents. Good work will stand you in good stead, so I take risks on certain people because I trust them to be well prepared and give an interesting audition.

An example of this was when I was casting a pilot drama called *Run*. The brief was to find black inner city London girls. I had seen an actor from Manchester in another production and thought she would be great. After seeing six or so good London girls, in came this girl from Manchester who blew them away – the dialogue was so fresh and different with a Mancunian accent. There was talk of changing the character, to make her from Manchester and how easily this could be done. Needless to say, she was well prepared and off the page.

One last thought that may seem like a minor thing, but it's not. Turn off your mobile phone while you're still in the waiting room – don't leave it until you're in the middle of your audition when it will be irritating and disruptive to break off and do it. You don't need it to appear busy and important. You are already important to us as we've invited you to this casting and we want you to be the one.

RECAP

- use your time before the audition wisely
- always ask the receptionist if there are any notes or script changes
- don't get distracted by anyone in the waiting room
- but if you do, then get out of the room
- turn off your mobile before you are called in

NEXT PLEASE

Finally you are called into the casting room and you are bursting to show us how good you are, how funny, how intelligent, how wonderful in every respect.

This is a common mistake that actors make. In fact, there's a massive misconception about what is actually happening in the casting process. Acting in castings and acting in a production of any kind, are two very different things.

We do not need to see how very very very good you are, we need to see that you can do what we are asking you to do. It's not about everything you can do, it's about doing what you've been asked to do and doing it well. An actor is only a cog in the very large machine that is the production. Of course your abilities and skills are important, but if all we've asked for is a wink and a smile, it's pointless hitting us with 40 lines of Shakespeare.

If I work with you for say 10-30 minutes in a casting, or even for four hours in a workshop, I can't begin to know how witty and clever you are, how great you are at certain things. I don't need to know the full range and depth of your abilities, I need to know that if a director gives you direction, you can do what you've been asked to do. If you ignore direction or fail to take it in because you're overexcited or hellbent on performing the way you prepared, then it's over.

I was casting Leona Lewis' *Better with Time* video with Sophie Muller. The idea was that the cast should look like an Italian film crew from the fifties/sixties. An actor, let's call him 'Tom', arrived looking perfectly dressed in trousers, white shirt and braces. He had read the script and had obviously prepared well. I threw a glance at Sophie to say he looks great, and she agreed. Tom was 90% there. I gave all the actors some direction: we were asking them to be a film crew and act in a very natural, realistic way. In the setup, Tom was to be the Director of Photography.

When I said "Action", Tom went for it. He was shouting at the other actors, directing them here and there, acting stressed and impatiently stamping his feet. It was a fullblown, over the top tour de force, and totally not required. I asked Sophie what she thought of him – she said that she loved his look but he hadn't listened to the direction at all and could possibly be a handful on set. That was it for Tom. Sophie knew it was going to be a busy shoot and there would no time to coax a performance out of him.

Shame, because even if Tom had just leaned motionless against the prop camera for the two-minute audition he would have got the gig. He basically acted his way out of a job, trying to show us everything he could do, all the wonderful facets of his ability, how he could be angry, stressed and over-emotional. All he really needed to do was act natural, as instructed.

So when you're in the casting suite, listen to the direction you're being given. If a director can't direct you, it's game over. In the theatre, there may be time to 'get you there' and the director may learn a lot about you during the six weeks of rehearsal. Film, tv and commercials are different. Shooting is expensive and there's usually very little rehearsal time.

What we really need to know from a casting is that you can be prepared, professional and that you have some ability. All the interesting ideas can come after you get the part.

Now if you have learned the script, please for the love of God put it to one side. Actors who keep the script in their hands throughout the audition drive me to distraction. Using the script as a crutch and clinging to it for dear life takes away from your performance. Trust yourself to know that you've memorised it and put it down.

You could probably reel off monologues you learned years ago and you've probably memorised hundreds of lines in your time. So why keep the script for a simple commercial tag line in your hand? So many actors break fine performances by referring to the script. If you're holding the script or it's in your line of sight, you will find yourself looking at it, so throw it to one side. Check it between takes by all means but don't break your performance. Most directors would rather you paraphrased the words than stop what you're doing to look at a line. Don't forget that your performance is being recorded for the people who will make the final decisions about the casting and we need to show them clean takes. So it's very beneficial for you not to refer to your script.

"Can you tell us your name and agent please, can we see your profiles please, can we see your hands . . ." Honestly, I've woken up muttering this phrase, it's basically our catchphrase like "Garlic bread!" or "Computer says no!" It's the ident before an audition and it's not some conspiracy or something casting directors do to justify their existence. We need to do idents for several reasons, mainly to establish a clear image of you so that we can check for skin blemishes or piercings for example, and to check your hands in case a closeup is needed.

The ident may also be the first shot our client sees of you, so try not to be bored or surly. I know it can make you feel as if you're in a processing plant but it's important, so try and make it pleasant.

You've done your ident, and now it's time to act. But before you ever do a take in any type of audition, you should always ASK A QUESTION.

The reason I tell actors to do this is because asking a question helps you build a relationship with the director. It immediately identifies you as a person and not just the fifth or the twenty-fifth actor of the day. It's good advice that holds true for any job interview, and asking something like "How did you start in this business?" will invite an answer from your interviewer. Hopefully a conversation will kick off and a connection will be established that leaves a good impression. As I've said, a casting is a job interview and the same theory applies.

Asking a question of the director or casting director will get them directly conversing with you. Sometimes you'll go into a room and the director is jetlagged or bored or just plain rude, so a direct question may jolt them into some interaction.

A good, solid question that will never go against you is "How should I pitch my performance? Are you looking for a natural or a heightened performance?" The answer to this simple question is extremely important to you. No matter how much information you've already been given, it's still hard to pitch your performance. You may only get one take and you don't want to waste it under or over-performing.

If you have any questions at all about the script, ask them. Without a full understanding of what it is you're supposed to be doing, you'll be stabbing in the dark. I've seen many actors do take after take when it's clear they need to ask a question about it. Some actors even feel they shouldn't be asking any questions in an audition. This is ridiculous. It's your audition, your time, and your career so take charge and ask questions if you need to know something. Don't waste a take or an audition by being meek!

Be mindful of everything else you say in the casting room. Try not to mock the material, whatever you may privately think about it. There may be ad agency creatives and producers present and rubbishing the script or the product is a good way to talk yourself out of a job. You may think "I would never do that" but I've seen it happen so many times and will no doubt continue to see it. You might even be joking about the product on tape before your take and then there's no time to edit it out. It happens.

RECAP

- it's not about what you can do but what you've been asked to do
- listen to the direction
- learn the script then put it aside
- give a pleasant ident
- always ask a question
- don't mock the material

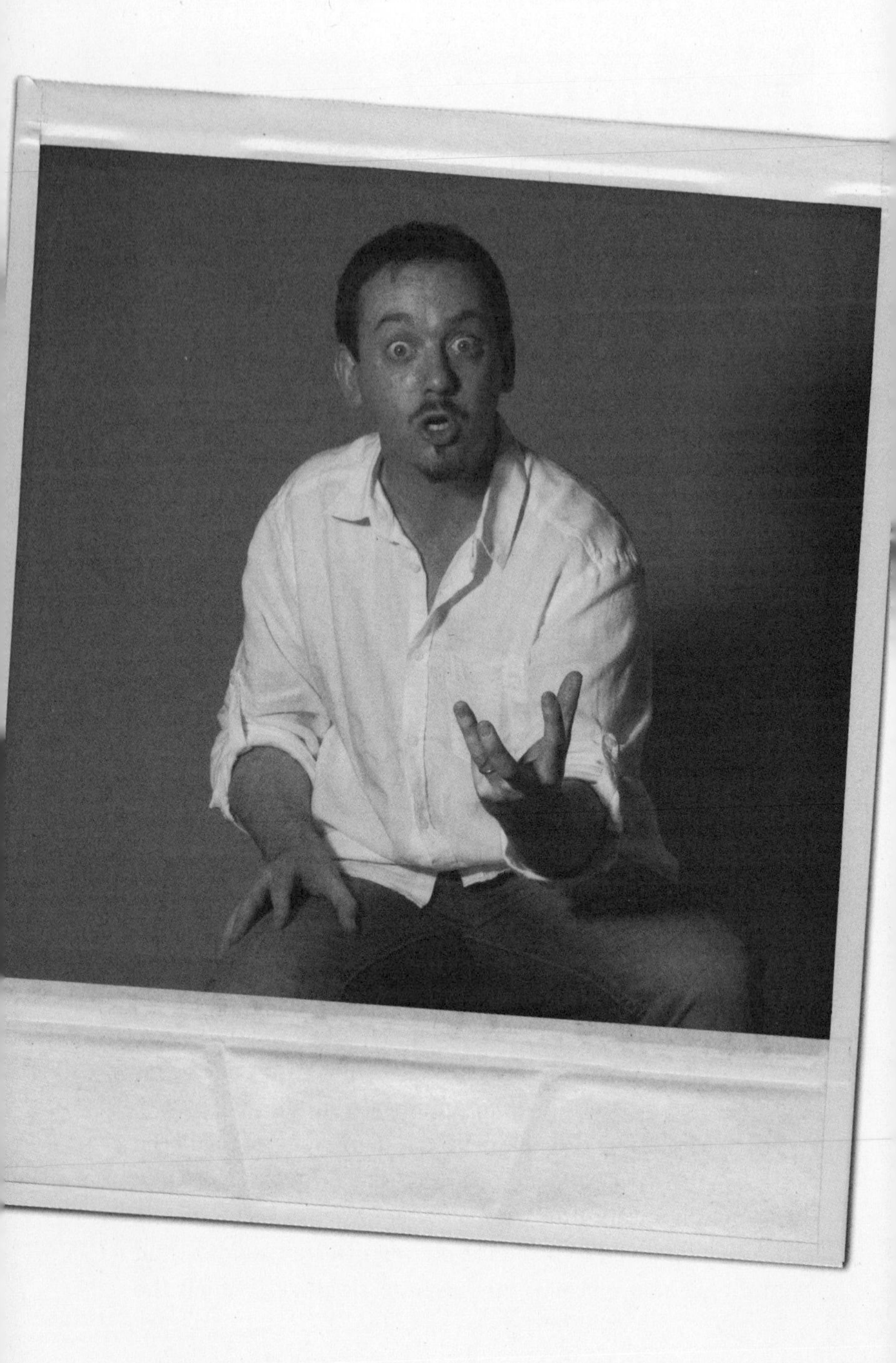

JUST IMPROVISE IT

In some auditions you've been to the director will tell you to "Just improvise it". This can be a terrible freedom. Being asked to improvise a script or idea seems fantastic to an actor, but much of the time what we see is overacting, overcomplication and generally running wild.

My advice when asked to improvise is to keep it simple and keep it as close as possible to the idea in the script.

A script for a tv commercial will have been tightly storyboarded with every shot and word of dialogue approved by the time it gets to the casting stage. So if you're now reading this script and it says "Man picks up phone, says hello and smiles" then just give them that in the audition. Don't bombard everyone with witty asides and minutes of improvised dialogue. Keep your improvisation close to the script because when your audition tape is shown it needs to reflect what has already been pitched by the agency. If an actor is giving it his all but it's irrelevant to the script, then it's a wasted audition.

Remember that you are acting on camera and the camera needs to see what you are doing. Some actors lose control when they're improvising and meander around aimlessly, mistaking high energy and tomfoolery for a good performance. This is what I call 'actor masturbation' – the actor is enjoying himself, but no-one else is. It happens when an actor throws energy into a performance without thinking about its relevance to the script. The actor thinks that he's put in a marvellous performance but nothing is communicated to the audience.

I once auditioned for an Austrian bank commercial. The idea was that two painters, one middle-aged and one young, had to paint a wall. I took the older actor's part and ignoring the direction given to us by the casting director, we did what we thought was a very funny piece of slapstick. We left the studio well pleased with ourselves. “See you in Austria” we said. How wrong we were. I later found out that what was needed was a subtle performance and the casting tape was of no use to the director. We just hadn’t listened.

RECAP

- keep improvisation simple
- keep improvisation close to the script
- avoid self-indulgent irrelevance

THE RECALL

Well done! You've got a recall. Pat yourself on the back because that means you've done a good audition. Casting directors keep notes on the good people, especially those who are recalled. Making your way into a casting director's notebook is a surefire way to get more auditions.

I like nothing better than meeting a new actor who impresses me. I then start to think about what else I could see them for. Don't forget that a casting director could be working on several projects simultaneously.

Here are some basic questions you should ask your agent or the casting director before your recall.

1. Are there any script changes or a new script?
Obviously you don't want to be handed a new script just as you get to the recall. The stress of having to learn something in a such a short time can hold you back while auditioning. So get the new script or script changes beforehand.

2. Are there any notes from the director or casting director?
Check if you should be wearing something different to the casting. Ask if the director has any notes or directions on your performance, however subtle.

3. Are you being recalled for the same role?
Sometimes you can be recalled for another role in the production. If this is the case, you may need to see different dialogue and wear different clothes. The shoot date may now be different, so recheck your availability.

Unless otherwise instructed you should wear the same outfit to the recall that you wore in the initial meeting. It could be counterproductive to dress or wear your hair in a different way.

We recall actors for a variety of reasons. It could be to hone your performance or perhaps we didn't get enough footage in the first session. If there have been script changes, we have to film you with new dialogue. The recall might even be your first meeting with the director as they may not have attended the first casting session. The client may want to come to the recall and make a decision about the actors. We may have a special outfit for you to wear.

For recall auditions there can be a lot of bodies in the room. In the case of commercials, the room is usually full of agency creatives, account managers and producers. If it's film or tv, there may be executive producers, department heads, commissioning editors and studio bosses in attendance.

I know it can be intimidating but keep focused and seek out the director. The director will be the one who guides your performance. The director will be the one fighting your corner to get you cast. So stick with the director, take on board the instructions and above all follow the direction.

If you don't get the job after being recalled, don't let it get to you. Shake it off and move on. It's a part of what you do so don't take it personally if you don't get cast this time.

Again, use your time in the waiting room wisely and don't forget to congratulate yourself when you come out – you've done a good audition and it's a great advertisement for you.

RECAP

- ask basic questions about any changes or notes
- wear the same outfit to the recall
- keep focused and seek out the director
- move on if you don't get it this time

WHAT A CASTING DIRECTOR DOES

At a basic level my job is very simple. I have to bring in the best people to audition for a role. I have to give the director options for each and every role. I have to make sure the actors are prepared and comfortable. I have to assist in getting the best performance from the actors.

A casting director does not represent actors. That might seem obvious to most of you but I've often been asked by actors to represent them.

A casting director is not out to block your performance, stop you performing or dislike you in any way.

Casting directors want you to be brilliant, we want you to be fantastic and we want you to do the best audition ever when you walk into that casting room. Why? Because if you are fantastic then we look fantastic. Doing a confident, well-prepared audition makes us look good. That's what it's all about. We want you to look great and we are here to help you look great.

The choice to bring in an actor is down to trust. We have to trust that you will do a good audition. How do we figure out if we can trust you?

It may be because we know your work and your good work speaks for itself. We may have seen you in something or auditioned you before and liked what you did. Just because you didn't get the part doesn't mean your audition was bad. I sometimes disagree with directors and producers about the choice of actor. If they don't want you for the role, I'll make a note for myself to get you in for something else.

If we haven't met you before, we will review your credits and look at the people you've worked for and what level you've performed at. Your credits will show the trust that has been put by others in your abilities. I might bring you in after a recommendation from your agent, depending on their standing in the industry.

And there will be times when I may not recognise your credits and don't know the people you've worked with, but I'll take a chance on you. I'll do this when I'm working on a job where there's no client present, and it's a great way for me to meet new actors.

Actors always say to me "But it's all about the look isn't it?" It's true in some instances, for example if a multinational has specified brunettes for their advertising campaign or if there's a requirement to cover various social demographics. Watching directors at work though I find that this is less and less often the case. It's the actor's performance and the actor's relationship with the director, however brief, that informs the director's choice. What matters is your craft and your focus on the task in hand. Don't worry about 'the look'.

It may also be my job to provide direction in a casting session. Always listen to the casting director or assistant – they will brief you on the exact performance the director wants.

Actors also say to me that it seems to be the same leading actors in everything, and wonder why they are not getting seen for bigger roles. Sometimes those 'leading actors' are not really leading actors, but we may need a name in the part for marketing or financial reasons. Big budgets and big fees can require big names to front a production. And then there are times when a virtually unknown actor is cast in a major role. So don't fret about the size of the role, just do it to the best of your ability.

Casting directors don't usually make the final decision as to who gets the part. But we do have influence and we will fight your corner, so give us a great performance to fight for. You need to be prepared so you hit the ground running when you come to meet us.

RECAP

- casting directors want you to give the best audition ever
- if <u>you</u> look good, you make <u>us</u> look good
- we can influence the final decision and we're here to help you

A FEW ACTING TIPS

It's said that we learn from our mistakes. As an actor I made many mistakes. Please feel free to learn from mine.

I was lucky as a young actor. I did four big auditions in a row and got all four of the jobs. The first was for *The War of the Buttons*, next was for *Angela's Ashes*, then it was my entrance audition for Trinity College, Dublin, followed by *Rebel Heart* for the BBC. I was basically four for four, perfect score, and in my naivety I thought that the acting industry was easy. I thought that I was fully developed at 18 and that I could do no wrong with a script. I just did what I always did: throw loads of energy and intensity into the role. Or simply stare intensely until my eyes watered! I was feeling it, therefore it was good, when really all I was doing was actor masturbation. I would add intense emotion that was not there because it made it interesting to me. I ignored punctuation, stage directions and sometimes the director in favour of the way I felt the scene should be. I was cocky, arrogant, completely unprepared and ill informed.

The audition that stands out now as a prime example of my naivety was for Martin Scorsese's *Gangs of New York* with the American casting director Ellen Lewis in Dublin. Instead of focusing on the script I'd been given, I daydreamed about working with Scorsese and DiCaprio. I read the entire script – my character was a member of a gang of poor street thieves. Instead of looking rather quirky or scruffy for the audition, I gelled my hair, wore my Saturday night best and attempted to look as handsome as I could. Now I'll be honest and admit that it's a lot easier for me to look mad, quirky or scruffy than it is to look handsome. But that was the decision I made.

I remember going in and feeling nervous about meeting such a high-profile casting director, and I think I was also nervous because I knew in my heart of hearts that I hadn't prepared properly. I ended up doing a disjointed, stop-start, over the top audition . . . I mean, this is Scorsese and I'm channelling Charles Hawtrey! I only got two takes and although I told myself I could get a recall I knew it was rubbish.

Analysing that audition I know I was underprepared. Instead of concentrating on the script I met a friend for coffee beforehand, wasting vital prep time and interrupting my focus. I didn't pay attention to the character in the script and didn't dress to look like a gang member, I just thought about how I wanted to look in the audition. I should have looked dishevelled like I'd come from a dirty New York ghetto, instead I smelled nice and was clean shaven as if I was about to meet my new girlfriend's nice middle class parents.

The reason I dressed up in my best clothes was because I had a vision of myself that was a complete misrepresentation. In retrospect I see that I had succeeded in getting acting gigs because I was playing characters close to my type – quirky and Irish. But I started to rebel against this because I saw myself as a leading man or supervillain because these were the characters I wanted to play or because of the actors who had influenced me. It seems farcical now, but that's how I wanted my career to progress. Instead of embracing what talents and assets I actually had, I was pitching myself differently and thus neutralising these assets. I was making myself normal and uninteresting. I was not a six-foot leading man with a strong chin, neither was I an intelligent-sounding supervillain.

As an actor, you need to know what your assets are and you need to embrace them. Play your type and play it well, then casting directors will begin to see how solid your work is and perhaps start thinking of you for roles of a different type.

To figure out what your assets are, you have to be honest with yourself. If you are fat you are fat, if you are plain you are plain, if you are beautiful you are beautiful. Whatever you are will, in some way, restrict you. Play to your strengths and good performances will stand to you.

I ignored a lot of very vital lessons when I did drama at university because I felt I was the finished article. I mainly read drama for the university experience, and felt that because of my successes I knew better than my lecturers and that I could adapt myself to any role with little work. I was very wrong to think this.

Before I started my university course, I was advised to work hard to neutralise my strong Limerick accent by Ros Hubbard and my then agent Lisa Anne Porter. I understood why they were advising me to do this, but because of my lazy work ethic and 'know it all' mentality I did little work on this aspect of my craft. I didn't set aside enough time to learn accents and I did little to enhance my vocal capacity. Drama school is a very safe environment in which to hone your craft, take risks and develop your vocal range. My craft suffered because I didn't take advantage of this opportunity and failed to embrace my assets.

I saw myself as a camera actor and wasn't worried about developing my vocal capacity, but this attitude did not cut it in the real world of the jobbing actor. I later auditioned for the part of a young Hitler in *The Rise of Evil*; my German accent was a truly terrible mix of Ringo Starr meets Inspector Clouseau. The fact that I had not exercised my voice or developed accents limited me as a performer.

As an actor you need to master the two very different crafts of camera and stage acting. It still amazes me the number of jobbing actors who have no concept of camera acting and play every performance to the back of the theatre, turning their faces away from the camera in castings while delivering key lines or hitting scenes with so much emotion that it comes across as hammy.

Sometimes it's hard to blame the actors. So much training

is still set in the Gielgud or Olivier era, with drama schools allocating very little time to camera acting. As I mentioned earlier, I've spoken to actors who've completed three-year courses with a mere week devoted to this essential aspect of the craft. When they come into the real world, 75% of their auditions involve a camera and if they cannot adjust their performances, the meetings are wasted. These actors are suddenly having to figure out how to hone their performances when really this should have been dealt with during their studies.

I was once casting the part of a judge for an Associated Rediffusion docudrama, and many of the actors were in their seventies. Many had obviously been trained for the stage and only met a camera when auditioning, or had few tv credits on a largely theatrical CV. Others had varied CVs with good television and film roles as well as theatre parts. The three actors who were shortlisted had nicely varied careers; none with mainly theatre credits had been considered. We had asked for a natural performance, subtle and realistic, but those actors with CVs loaded with theatre work had given us all-encompassing, over the top auditions. Some of them had over 50 years experience in the business but couldn't grasp the difference between stage and camera acting. Knowing the difference is an invaluable asset for the jobbing actor.

For camera auditions, remember that you should speak at a conversational level. Supposing the scene takes place between two friends at a dinner table. When you're having a meal with someone in real life, you don't project like crazy or turn on your acting voice. So speak in a normal tone – there's no need to project. When we watch a film we are seeing a slice of another world, another life. There are microphones so that the actors don't have to project their voices. So don't feel you have to project in a casting studio.

Another vital aspect of camera acting is listening to the other actor. It's very noticeable when an actor is not listening to another performer – we start to lose the sense of the text and the scene. An actor will compensate for not listening by adding pre-rehearsed reactions or gestures.

Listening, really listening on camera can be a beautiful thing to behold. If you are genuinely listening, the text you deliver back will make more sense and sound authentic. Many actors believe that the most important part of acting is their lines. This is a mistake. If you watch actors like Kevin Spacey, Steve McQueen or Daniel Day Lewis, their strongest moments are when they are listening, reacting, waiting to deliver dialogue. Steve McQueen would get a script and immediately start crossing out dialogue and replace it with silent reaction, just listening to what's happening in the scene.

When you are listening properly you don't need to push reactions. If you are really listening then the reactions will happen naturally. If you see a person on the bus who looks depressed, it's not because they're sitting there thinking "I'm depressed, I'm depressed, I'm depressed so I must put on my depressed look", it's because they're feeling blue and it shows on the face without having to force it.

The face is an amazing instrument when an actor is on camera. It shows instantly what the actor is thinking or feeling, be it angry, shocked, upset or happy. There's no need to telegraph or force facial expressions for the camera. All you need to do is LISTEN AND THINK IT. The emotion will appear on your face effortlessly. The best acting lesson I ever had was from David Puttnam who told me to "Think something in your tummy and it will appear on your face."

Forcing expressions or reactions on camera looks awful. Overacting is a terrible thing, and most of the time you won't even realise you are doing it if you're too self-involved. Obviously if you're acting in something, usually comedy, that requires you to act over the top, then go for it, but still be aware of projecting your voice too much.

RECAP

- know your type, know your assets and embrace them
- master the differences between stage and camera acting
- no need to project to camera
- listen, really listen, and your feelings will show on your face

YOUR AUDITION IS AN ADVERTISEMENT FOR YOU

As an actor, you are in charge of your career. That means you are in charge of your advertising, business affairs, training and development, and the final product – you.

An agent is there to help you get auditions, advise you, help get your name around and do the deal. But you also have to be proactive in getting your name, showreel and invitations out there. You can't leave it all to your agent.

I was terrible at advertising and self-promotion when I was an actor. I left everything to my agent and wondered why I wasn't getting lots of auditions. My success had made me lazy and I would sit around waiting for the phone to ring when I should have been sending letters or emails to casting directors, theatre companies, directors and producers.

By advertising I mean that you need to send out your CV and invitations to your performances. We can't know that you exist unless you tell us. We may have come across your CV on Spotlight or seen you in the theatre or on tv, but you stand more chance of being noticed if you invite casting directors to see your work.

I know it can be soul destroying to send out hundreds of emails or letters and get no response, but I guarantee that it is always worth the effort. I have seen random CVs land on casting directors' desks, my own included, that have suited a brief and suddenly that actor gets an audition. I may not respond to every CV and invitation, otherwise my days would consist of writing replies, but I do read everything and file it for future reference. I prefer to receive CVs and links to CVs by email, but check a casting director's website to find out how they like to receive submissions.

Cold calling can sometimes work. You may even get a

meeting or audition out of it, but more often than not it can be frustrating both for you and the casting director. Your call probably won't be put through. I may not want to break off what I'm doing. It's best to write or email.

The internet is a real blessing for actors. Never before have actors had so many free and inexpensive tools to help promote themselves and advertise their abilities.

These days, it's a very simple matter to sign up for a free blog at somewhere like WordPress or tumblr, and upload images, MP3 voice files, video clips and CV notes. It's easy to update your blog with information about the productions you're currently involved in. If you're feeling more adventurous, you could register a domain name and create your own site with free design software. If you don't want to create a site or blog then at the very least upload your showreel to YouTube or MySpace.

It's incredibly useful for me if actors have put their work online so that I can look through images and showreels – it can inform my decision instantly without having to wait for a DVD in the post, by which time it may be too late, and the session may already be filled. An actor with a website or blog shows a certain professionalism and respect for their craft and career.

When you're compiling a voice reel, it's a good idea to begin with a few moments of your normal voice. Not every project will require your best R.P. delivery and it's good for us to hear the real you. One of the best reels I've heard recently started with the actor in his own accent telling us details of the London to Birmingham train service. It was utterly dull and normal, which made it fantastically memorable.

Aim to include a variety of clips that demonstrate the range and tones of your voice. If you're good at accents then showcase this talent. Here's a sample running order:

1. Introduce yourself in your normal voice
2. A fast-paced, high-energy, hard-sell commercial
3. A serious finance commercial with R.P.
4. A smooth and sexy beer commercial
5. A documentary voiceover or a chapter from an audio book

The voicereel should be about three minutes in length as we usually only need snippets to know if you can do what is required. But it's useful to keep longer readings of certain deliveries in case more audio is needed. Supply your agent with your voice work as MP3 files so that they're readily available, and keep copies on your hard drive or memory stick so that they can be instantly emailed.

Your showreel should present the best of the work you have done. I am often asked 'how long should my showreel be?' The standard is three to five minutes but if you have a lot of nonsense why stretch it out? It's not a problem to have a showreel that is a minute long provided that minute shows you in a good light. A casting director will watch as much as they need to make their decision about you. I sometimes only need about 30 seconds depending on the project to make my decision. As a casting director I use showreels for various reasons. Sometimes I need a showreel to get a sense of your physique or your voice quality; sometimes I need to see how good a performer you are or can be. Some actors don't like using footage from commercials, but if the footage is good and gives a good representation of your craft then you should use it. Ask people their opinions on the pieces you are considering using. I don't advocate spending lots of money on a glossy showreel; I don't think anyone has ever been cast because their showreel was well edited with a good backing track . . . I'll watch a grainy VHS as long as I can see you act! Ordinary laptops and PCs all come with some movie editing software so

DIY it. Remember we are looking at the quality in the content not how the content is put together.

If you don't have any clips from productions you have been in, you might have a friend who can shoot your monologue or you could hire a cameraperson, perhaps an aspiring director. Don't try too hard with the camera angles or background. Don't let your mate talk you into building a set or adding strange lighting because they're on some Tarantino trip. Trying to be clever almost always ends up looking cheap, nasty and amateurish.

Lock the camera off at a mid to tight closeup and shoot against a plain background. Choose a monologue and deliver it straight to camera. Ignore any thrills or frills that will detract from your performance. Keeping it simple will help us to focus on you.

Actors who have done nothing but theatre work say they find it hard to compile a showreel. This shouldn't be the case. Thousands of short films get shot every year in Britain and I highly recommend doing them, even if it's just for the experience. You could find yourself working with a great up and coming director and get good clips for your reel.

It's true that some agents won't put you up for short films because there's little or no commission for them or they're sick of running around after film students. If you're looking to get footage it should be your job to find out where to get it.

Your headshot is obviously very important, but sometimes actors tie themselves in knots worrying about it. In my opinion, your work, your credits and your craft tell me more about you. All the headshot has to be is a good representation of you, preferably in closeup with minimal makeup and free of clutter like earrings and labels.

I once had a headshot done wearing a godawful woollen jumper. You couldn't help but focus on this awful jumper. My agent laughed so hard when she saw the prints that she almost broke something.

Finally, it's very difficult to be an actor in the UK without being a member of Spotlight. I use it all the time to source actors for projects and so does every other casting company I've ever worked with. The Spotlight Directory is the industry standard.

And you can't be an actor in the UK without *Contacts*. As I mentioned at the beginning of this book, *Contacts* is the actor's bible. It's full of helpful information, plus contact details for agents, casting directors, studios and photographers. It really is a must for actors who are starting out.

RECAP

- don't leave everything to your agent
- be proactive in your self-promotion
- get your work online
- keep your headshot simple
- join Spotlight and get Contacts

WHAT DO YOU WANT FROM THIS?

Before becoming an actor you need to think about what you want from life. I was increasingly unhappy with the idea of being a 'struggling actor' and realised that I wanted a more steady, stable life. I remember the day it dawned on me that my heart was no longer in it. I was unhappy doing a part-time bar job and getting the odd audition, so I had started working full time as an assistant at Hubbard Casting. I had just moved into a new flat with friends from university and the Hubbards were allowing me time off for auditions, which were mostly for commercials. Instead of seeing these as a great opportunity to advertise my craft and impress a director, I was finding them frustrating, unrewarding and dull. Then I was offered a small part in a play that would tour the provincial theatres for several months and 'possibly transfer to the West End'.

I was unexcited about doing this. I didn't want to give up my job and my new flat. I was enjoying being a casting director and learning lots about the industry day by day. The fact that I was uninterested and unexcited told me everything I needed to know. The acting bug had gone. I was becoming self-conscious and inhibited during my auditions and preparing less and less for them. If the job wasn't going to pay well, then I was uninterested and didn't even turn up to the casting. What I should have been doing was trying to get student film or fringe theatre experience to keep me busy and out there.

People choose to be actors for many reasons. Some want the glamour, some want the attention, some love the spoken word and want to communicate with an audience. I am amazed when I meet people who have given up professional careers in law and accounting to become actors, but why not? If you think this is where your happiness lies, then give it a try.

Your decision to become an actor should not be taken

lightly. It's not easy and it's not all loving applause and premieres. It's worth repeating that only a small percentage of actors make a decent living while the majority work at other jobs, hoping to get the elusive break. And the handful of actors who do make a good living are the ones with the best prepared auditions.

There are many reasons why people don't make it in the industry. Some plainly have no talent. Some have a misconception about who they are and what they can bring to a role. Some may have great talent but lose their patience and give up when it seems that it's not going to happen for them.

As an actor you need to have a keen awareness of who you are and what you can bring. I had a massive misconception of how I perceived myself and how others perceived me. You can use whatever you are, just don't consider yourself to be something you're not. And if you're not comfortable with yourself, then others won't be comfortable with you.

Above all, strong well prepared auditions will stand you and your career in great stead. It's your career and your craft so have the confidence to take control of the audition. Because that's what it's all about.

Just remember, it's the audition, stupid!

PART THREE:

ASK BRENDAN

Should I work as an extra?

If it's early on in your career, then it's probably a good thing. And it's very useful if you don't have any camera experience or film/tv credits on your CV.

You'll gain on-set experience which shows initiative and respect for your craft. You may also make valuable connections with other actors and crew.

Extra work is good money, and you never know, you may be seen or noticed or even get a line. You won't get these things in a call centre.

What if extra work is the only work I'm getting?

If after a few years you're still doing nothing but extra work, then you need to address this, unless of course you're happy with the situation.

What other part time jobs are good?

Industry-related work is ideal. Drop your regular work CV into casting studios, production companies and theatres. Part time work in places like these will help you keep your ear to the ground, and you may even pick up the odd part. I've had casting assistants pick up commercial parts just by filling in for a late or cancelled actor.

As with extra work, if you stay as a casting assistant for too long, it will alter the way a casting director sees you. Make it clear that you are still acting and you can only commit on a part time basis.

If you're in a situation where you must work to pay the rent and bills, then an evening job is usually better than daytime work as it will leave you free for auditions.

Do I need more than one agent?

If you're an actor with model good looks, then it's an advantage to have a model agent as well as your acting agent. But you need to be clear about who is putting you forward for what to avoid double-booking issues.

There's no advantage to having two or more agents for commercial and background work. They will all – inevitably – suggest you for the same projects, which doesn't make you look very good.

If you're not native to the country, having an agent in your homeland to put you forward for local projects is a situation where having two agents could be beneficial to you.

Should I move to get better opportunities?

It's true that a bigger city offers more opportunities, but if you feel that you're not getting enough work or auditions the chances are that this won't change in a new place.

Address the essential issues first – knowing who you are, playing to your strong points and preparing well for auditions. A poor work ethic means that you will be fighting a losing battle wherever you are.

If you are getting work – in Dublin for example – but feel you've outgrown the place, then this is also not a good reason to move. My advice is to stick with it. You can always fly to London for casting calls and your good work will speak for itself.

I get told that many UK agents insist that you are permanently based in London. It's simply not true. As an actor you should be free to go where the work is at a moment's notice.

But I've moved anyway. Now what?

My best advice is try not to get tied into a long rental lease. Stay with friends or relatives first and test the waters, figure out if you like the place. Get yourself a part time job and keep yourself busy rather than sitting around getting depressed. Trust me, a big new city where you don't know many people can be very daunting.

What's my casting type and how do you see me?

Please don't ask me. I just met you five minutes ago and I don't know you. I don't focus on it, and neither should you.

No matter what you do, something about you will exclude you from getting a role, in the same way that something about you will help you get it. Pink hair will stop you getting some parts and land you others.

Take whatever auditions you can, concentrate on that and don't worry about other things that only distract you from the work.

to ask Brendan a question go to

→ www.itstheauditionstupid.com
or
→ www.facebook.com/itstheauditionstupid

PART FOUR:

RESOURCES

USEFUL WEBSITES

As I've already mentioned, the internet is a fantastic tool for an actor. Whether it's having your own website or your showreel on YouTube, or using it to research a role, the internet is awesome for an actor. It's also a great place to find work, workshops, agents, theatre open days and so on.

I have listed a few useful websites that you may or may not be aware of, but there are many more. So it's up to you to get on the internet and find helpful websites, links, forums and blogs. After all, it's your career, so get searching . . .

→ `www.spotlight.com`

Actor directory, industry leader. The Spotlight publication *Contacts* which is updated annually is a must have for every actor. Spotlight also advertise workshops and Q&A sessions, and have a fantastic advice centre.

→ `www.uk.castingcallpro.com`

Actor directory, similar to Spotlight. Casting Call Pro gives actors a listing in their directory of actors, accessible to thousands of casting professionals, theatre and production companies. You can also network with other actors and browse their industry resources database which includes information on hundreds of agents and photographers.

→ `www.thecastingwebsite.com`

Actor directory, catering for younger actors, very good regional contacts. Ideal if you are starting out as a young actor and not London based. Working with local youth theatres, The Casting Website is dedicated to the social development of its members. It helps educate young performers, parents and local youth groups as to the importance of training and the social and educational benefits of being a part of this exciting industry. The Casting Website has a keen, energetic team that are fantastic at advising young talent.

→ `www.equity.org.uk`

Actors' Union, advice on fees and actors' rights. Equity is the UK trade union for professional performers and creative practitioners. Whether you have an agent or not, Equity can help and advise you on your rights as a performer.

→ `www.actorscentre.co.uk`

Centre devoted to further training of actors, and advice. The Actors Centre was created by actors, for actors. It provides ongoing training giving actors the opportunity to enhance every aspect of their craft.

→ `www.fringereport.com`

Up to date information on fringe theatre festivals. Its reviews section will keep you informed on what smaller theatre companies are up to. You can also see what festivals are coming up and research who is involved and where to send your CV.

→ `www.stagework.org.uk`

Jobs in and around the theatre, info on workshops and

lectures. Like Fringe Report it gives details on up and coming festivals so you can get your CV in early.

→ `www.skillset.org`

Industry jobs in front of and behind camera. Skillset is the industry body which supports skills and training for people in creative media. If you can't get an acting gig then you can possibly get part-time work on a set or in a production office.

→ `www.mandy.com`

Industry jobs in front of and behind camera. Mandy also posts casting calls for lots of short films and feature films.

→ `www.shootingpeople.org`

Industry jobs in front of and behind the camera with emphasis on independent film making. Good for networking and picking up short film info.

→ `www.productionbase.co.uk`

Industry jobs in front of and behind camera. More focused on behind the camera but still good if you're looking for a few weeks' work.

→ `www.pcrnewsletter.com`

PCR – Production Casting Report – is a guide to auditions and castings calls in the world of film, television and theatre. Aimed at actors, technicians and agents, it provides an insight into the very latest productions.

→ `www.thepma.com`

Acting agents' association, gives a definitive list of all the accredited agents.

→ `www.drama.ac.uk`

Drama school listings and theatre training information. A useful website if you want to investigate the drama schools that are out there.

→ `www.ncdt.co.uk`

The National Council for Drama Training is a partnership of employers in theatre, broadcast and media industries, employee representatives and training providers. This website will give you a list of accredited drama courses.

→ `www.getintotheatre.org`

The Arts Council site with information on careers in theatre.

→ `www.cdet.org.uk`

Council for Dance Education and Training, with information on training in all forms of dance.

→ `www.nayt.org.uk`

The National Association of Youth Theatres. This website gives young people and parents information on getting into theatre, whether it's to join a local youth theatre or a career in the industry as an actor, writer, director or technician.

→ www.oldvictheatre.com/ovnv/

Old Vic New Voices (OVNV) aims to support emerging talent, inspire young people and open up The Old Vic Theatre to new and diverse audiences. The Old Vic has open auditions every year to find new talent. You just have to register to be seen. There are other large theatres that have similar open days, but as this is your career it's up to you to investigate and find them.

you can also find these
and other links at
→ www.itstheauditionstupid.com

CV AND COVER LETTER

Your CV should be concise and clear. If you can keep it to one page, that's great, but if not, then make sure the standout credits are on the front page.

Name
Contact information [double check it's correct!]
Credits
Skills

The cover letter should be short and to the point. I have never cast anyone because they wrote me a well-structured, witty letter.

Contact information [your own/agents]
Date

Dear Mr McNamara,

My name is John Smith. Please find enclosed my picture and CV. I would be delighted to be considered for any future projects.

Kind regards,
John Smith

These are the basics, but you could also include a line in the letter about a project or training you're currently involved in or have just completed.

THE SEVEN DEADLY SINS OF AUDITIONS

Here's a useful summary of the most common mistakes I see when auditioning actors. If you can eliminate these 'deadly sins', then you will be able to get ahead of the game.

1. NOT LISTENING

Actors not listening when the director or casting director is giving instructions. If you don't follow the direction given, then the game is up. Your vision of how a piece should be performed or the way you've rehearsed it may be completely different from what the director wants.

2. NOT LEARNING YOUR LINES

This will always work against you. Producers will worry that there's a problem here. Performing without the script will always look better on camera.

3. NOT WEARING THE APPROPRIATE CLOTHES

It's not about looking your best. Think about the role you are auditioning for and dress appropriately.

4. FOOT IN MOUTH SYNDROME

Shut up, shut up and shut up already. Be careful of what you say and to whom you say it. Don't risk it by being snide or overly familiar. In commercials, don't slag off the product or rubbish the script. Don't start asking about dates and confirmation at the end of the audition – leave that to your agent.

5. NOT UNDERSTANDING OR ASKING A QUESTION

If you don't get it or don't understand what you are being asked to do, then don't do the take. ALWAYS ASK A QUESTION if you are unclear.

6. LATE, LATE, LATE

Please try to be on time, even if that means getting to the casting location early and hanging around in a cafe. You are working against yourself if you are late, as before, the producer may wonder if there's a problem with you. If you're unavoidably running late, ring us and warn us, as a courtesy.

7. LEAVE IT AT THE DOOR

It's unprofessional to bring your personal problems and bad mood in to the room. If you're really in a bad way emotionally, perhaps it's best to stay at home this time.

AND ONE MORE

An extra one that's worth remembering. Don't bring your dog or baby into the audition room. They will probably steal the show.

ACKNOWLEDGMENTS

I would like to acknowledge John, Ros, Amy and Dan Hubbard for giving me a start as an actor and also the opportunity to work in this industry. Your generosity and kindness will never be forgotten.

I would like to thank my brothers Eamonn and Diarmuid, and my sisters Maria and Shirley for all their love and support.

A big thank you to my Limerick and Trinity lads for keeping me sane.

Thank you to the following casting directors and industry colleagues for the work, help, advice and support they have given me: Andrew Maclean and all at Coptic Studios, Rob McDonald and all at Die-Cast Studios, Lucy Ivison, Rose Wicksteed, Amanda Tabak, Sue Pocklington, Ali Fearnley, Will Davies, all at Spotlight, Rob Earnshaw and all at the Casting Website, James Heath, Liam Garvo, Michael McDonald, Andy Lartice, Tim Nunn, Neil Harris, Helen Littlewood and all at Smuggler, Jamie Thraves, Sophie Muller, Rob Small and all at Factory Films, Elliot Naftalin, Theresa Larche, Jess aan de Wiel, Nick Crawford, Pete Ryan and all at Park Village, Julia Stefanidis in Hamburg, Phil Dupree and all at Hello Love, Bob Thompson, Brenda LeSeelleur, Lord Puttnam, Sir Alan Parker, The Fluid Druids, Oonagh Kearney, Lesley Manning, The Samuel Beckett Centre at Trinity College Dublin and CBS Sexton Street, Limerick.

Thank you to all the directors and producers I have worked with over the years.

Thank you to my publisher Martin Wagner and all at Pinter & Martin. Thanks to Jan Heron for editing so well and letting my voice be heard.

And finally to all the actors and agents I work with every day, you make my job so great xxx.

ABOUT THE AUTHOR

Casting Director Brendan McNamara has worked in casting since 1998. Starting as a runner at Hubbard Casting, Brendan was privileged to gain experience at one of the world's premier casting companies. He returned to Ireland to complete a degree in Drama and Theatre Studies at Trinity College, Dublin. After finishing his studies, he returned to Hubbard Casting working on projects such as *The Bourne Supremacy*, *Churchill: The Hollywood Years*, *Silver City* and *Omagh*. He was also casting assistant for two series of *Taggart*.

On leaving Hubbard Casting, Brendan freelanced for several other casting companies, working on TV shows like the BBC's *M.I. High*, *A Class Apart* and *That Summer's Day*. He also worked on music videos for The Streets and Franz Ferdinand, and TV commercial campaigns for Tiger Beer, Direct Line and the Royal Bank of Scotland.

Brendan formed Beach Casting in May 2007. Since its inception, the company has had early success in establishing a name for itself with projects like Katy Brand's *Big Ass TV Show* for ITV and *The Agent*, an independent British feature film directed by Lesley Manning and written by Martin Wagner.

Recently Brendan has cast an animated feature film for Warhammer 40K featuring Terence Stamp, Sean Pertwee and John Hurt, *The Secret World Of Sam King* for BEBO/Universal Records and new campaigns for NSPCC, McDonalds, Tesco and VW. He cast *Treacle Jr.*, an independent British feature film directed by Jamie Thraves starring Aidan Gillen and Tom Fisher, which won Best Film at Dinard in 2010. In 2010 Brendan co-founded Dresden Pictures, a production and film development company. The company's first film *The Why Men* was shot in April 2011.

Before he became a casting director, Brendan featured

as an actor in the Warner Bros film *The War of the Buttons* produced by David Puttnam, Paramount Pictures' *Angela's Ashes* directed by Alan Parker, and the BBC Productions *Rebel Heart*, *Paradise Heights* and *Brooklyn Bridge*.

keep in touch
→ www.itstheauditionstupid.com
and
→ www.facebook.com/itstheauditionstupid

NOTES: